THE YOUNG TRACK AND FIELD ATHLETE

COLIN JACKSON

Sit-up exercises

Long jump

Shot put

Hurdles

Discus standing throw

Shot put

Exercises with a medicine ball

With a foreword by Gwen Torrence

DK

A DK PUBLISHING BOOK

Project editor Fiona Robertson   **Art editor** Rebecca Johns
US editor Camela Decaire
Photography John Garrett
Picture research Sharon Southren
Production Charlotte Traill
Deputy editorial director Sophie Mitchell
Deputy art director Miranda Kennedy

The young athletes
Nathan Allen, Sholeh Anghaee, Josselyne Engele,
James Maudner, John Reid, Ruth Tchaparian

First American Edition, 1996
2 4 6 8 10 9 7 5 3 1

Published in the United States by
DK Publishing, Inc.,
95 Madison Avenue, New York, NY 10016

A catalog record is available from the Library of Congress.

ISBN 0-7894-0855-4 (hardcover)
ISBN 0-7894-0474-5 (paperback)

Color reproduction by Colourscan, Singapore
Printed by Graphicom in Italy

Contents

4
To all young athletes

6
Starting out

8
Warming up

10
Sprint drills

12
Starting the race

14
Training for longer distances

16
The relay

18
Hurdles

20
Triple jump

22
Long jump

24
High jump

26
Discus

28
Javelin and shot put

30
Combined events

32
Index and
Acknowledgments

To all young athletes

"WHETHER YOU RUN, JUMP, THROW, or hurdle, the enjoyment that the sport of track and field can bring you is lifelong. At any level, taking part in track and field events teaches you both discipline and responsibility and develops your physical and mental strength. I have been very fortunate to have competed all over the world and have been a member of two Olympic teams because of my involvement with track and the very important role it has played in my life. I hope that you enjoy reading *The Young Track and Field Athlete*. Remember that if you do your best in everything that you choose, you will always receive many rewards! "

"It takes lots of self-discipline, commitment, and energy to be a successful athlete."

"Track and field is rarely considered a team sport, but during the relay, we all work together to get the baton around the track as quickly as possible."

"Once you are in a race, you realize that all the hard training is worthwhile."

At the World Championships
Colin Jackson with the gold medal he won for the 110-m hurdles at the 1993 World Championships in Stuttgart. His time of 12.91 seconds set a new World Record.

"Track and field is great fun and has a tendency to keep you young in your outlook."

"You have to give each race everything you've got!"

Track and field's history

TRACK AND FIELD is the oldest form of organized sports. It is actually a collection of different sports events, and dates back to ancient times, when jumping, running, and throwing skills were vital for hunting and warfare. The first Olympic Games were held in 776 BC at Olympia, in Greece. The Games were held every four years in honor of the god Zeus. Many of the events in the modern Games have their roots in these ancient beginnings.

Ancient Games, Olympia
Runners in the original Olympic Games at Olympia, in ancient Greece, above, wore helmets and carried shields, but competed naked. At the first recorded Games, in 776 BC, there was only one event, the *stade* race. The number of events and the length of the Games gradually increased until they were abolished altogether in 393 AD.

First Olympic Committee
The first meeting of the International Olympic Committee (IOC), in 1896, is shown above. Seated on the left is Frenchman Baron Pierre de Coubertin, who founded the modern Olympics. Also present are representatives from Greece, Germany, the former Soviet Union, Czechoslovakia, Hungary, and Sweden.

Athens, 1896
One of the first competitions in the 1896 Olympics was the 100 m, above. It was won by Thomas Burke of the US, who completed it in 12.0 seconds. Burke is second from the left in the picture.

World record beater
Jesse Owens, above, set a remarkable record in the 1936 games in Berlin, Germany, by winning four gold medals within an hour for the 100 m, the 200 m, the long jump, and as a member of the 4 x 100-m relay team.

The opening ceremony
The Olympics are opened by a member of the host country's Royal Family or national government. At the opening ceremony, the Olympic flame is brought into the stadium by a team of relay runners who have carried it from Olympia. The 1992 ceremony in Barcelona, Spain, is shown left.

A stadium
A stadium is arranged so that both running (or track) and jumping and throwing (or field) events can take place at the same time. A modern track is oval-shaped, measures 400 m around, and has between six and ten lanes. The track surface is usually made of plastic or rubber, which makes it both weather-resistant and hard-wearing. The field events take place in the center of the track. This area is called the infield.

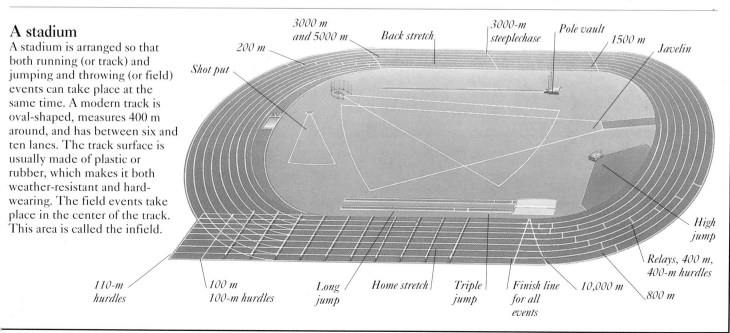

Shot put

200 m

3000 m and 5000 m

Back stretch

3000-m steeplechase

Pole vault

1500 m

Javelin

110-m hurdles

100 m 100-m hurdles

Long jump

Home stretch

Triple jump

Finish line for all events

10,000 m

800 m

Relays, 400 m, 400-m hurdles

High jump

Starting out

WHEN YOU FIRST START track and field sports, you will need comfortable clothes that allow you plenty of movement. Choose lightweight materials that are absorbent and easy to wash. The most important item is shoes. If you decide to continue in track and field, you will eventually need special shoes for each different event. However, to begin with, a pair of general-purpose sneakers, or "crosstrainers," will do. Ensure there is a layer of cushioning the length of the shoe to absorb the impact of running and jumping.

Boys' gear

For training, most boys wear a tank top that is tucked into shorts. The shorts should be loose enough to allow your legs to move freely. Most athletes have several tanks and shorts; a team or school set, or uniform, for competitions and at least one or two others for training. You can carry all your gear in a sports bag.

Shoes

Your shoes should be both comfortable and supportive. "Crosstrainers" or running shoes can be used for most athletic events. They do not have to be expensive, but they must fit well. Never buy shoes that are a size too big; you will find them difficult to run in and where they slip, they may cause painful blisters.

Make sure the tread on your soles is not worn.

Layer of cushioning

Note the wider shoulder strap on the girl's top.

Choose a sports bag that has a shoulder strap as well as handles.

Holes in the top allow air to circulate.

Cotton is the best material to wear because it absorbs sweat.

Cotton socks absorb sweat from your feet.

Always tie your laces properly, in a double knot if necessary.

Girls' gear

A girl's outfit is very similar to a boy's. However, girls' tops are wider at the shoulder and higher both at the front and under the arms. Many girls now wear leotards, which range from being high cut to knee length.

Tracksuit

Tracksuits are important, both in cold and warm weather. Whether you are training or competing, a lot of your time will be spent recovering, and your muscles must be kept warm to avoid strains and injuries. Tracksuits come in various materials from waterproof to light cotton. Make sure that the one you get is comfortable.

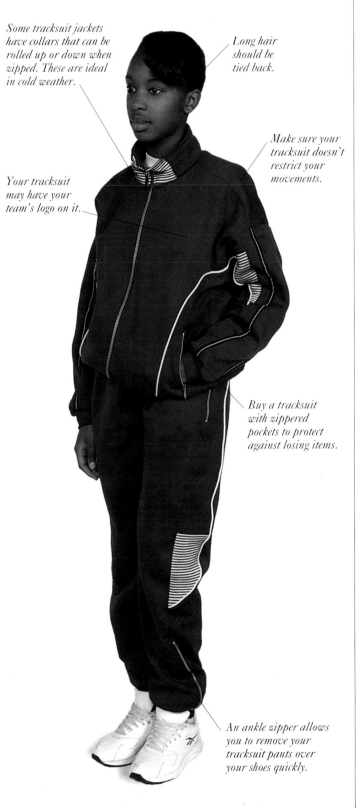

Some tracksuit jackets have collars that can be rolled up or down when zipped. These are ideal in cold weather.

Long hair should be tied back.

Make sure your tracksuit doesn't restrict your movements.

Your tracksuit may have your team's logo on it.

Buy a tracksuit with zippered pockets to protect against losing items.

An ankle zipper allows you to remove your tracksuit pants over your shoes quickly.

Joining a team

Before joining a team, you should visit the track and talk to other athletes and team officials to find out what the group offers. Make sure that there are coaches to give you training and that there will be competitions for your age group. Some teams provide a free uniform or free track use with their membership.

The minimum equipment that you need to join a group is a team uniform and proper shoes.

Many team tops have the team logo on them and that of the team's sponsor. There are often restrictions on the size of the lettering.

Teams often have registered colors for their gear.

Team uniforms must be worn in competitions.

Fasten your competition number to your top with safety pins.

Shorts usually match the team top.

Numbers

Competitors wear numbers on their chest and back so that they can be identified. High jumpers wear just one number on their chest, and pole vaulters have just one on their backs to avoid getting it caught on the bar.

Cleats

Cleats are used to provide a better grip on a track surface. They are much lighter than running shoes and provide less support. Choose a general pair for training and competing, such as a middle long-distance shoe, which has heel cushioning. Later on you may want a more specialized pair.

Cleats used on rubber tracks should be no more than 0.2 in (6 mm) long.

The cleats in these shoes are removable; always carry a spare set and wrench in case you lose one.

Warming up

BEFORE YOU TAKE PART in any kind of exercise, you must make sure that your muscles are warm and properly stretched. This keeps you flexible and prevents injury. Your warm-up should last for about 20 minutes. Begin with some gentle jogging to increase your body temperature and then do some stretching exercises. You should also go through a stretching routine after athletics. This allows your body to cool down properly and helps prevent stiffness the next day.

1 Look over your shoulder. Hold this position for a count of ten.

2 Bring your head back to the center position and rest.

3 Turn your head to the other side. With each stretch, try to go a bit farther.

Neck exercises

It is a good idea to begin your warm-up with neck exercises and work downward. This will make it easier to remember the sequence of exercises. Make sure you hold your neck in the stretch position during these exercises; never roll it.

1 Tilt your head toward your shoulder. Don't lift your shoulder up to your head.

2 Count to 10, relax, and then tilt to the other side.

3 Lower your chin to touch your chest. Remember to keep your shoulders back.

Arm circling

The muscles in the shoulders are connected to those in the chest. Exercises for one of these areas can therefore also benefit the other area. This exercise loosens the muscles in the arms and shoulders.

Your arms should pass close to your ears at the top of the swing.

Keep your arms straight throughout this exercise.

1 Start with your arms by your sides and your feet shoulder-width apart for balance. Keep your arms straight and slowly swing them backward.

Your legs should be slightly bent.

Feet should be shoulder-width apart.

Don't let your body move backward or forward during this exercise.

Keep your back straight.

2 Keep your arms straight as you swing them up past your head and down toward the ground in a big circle.

Try to breathe normally; don't try to keep pace with the swings.

Bring your arms close to your hips at the bottom of the swing.

3 When your body begins to feel looser, change direction and swing your arms from front to back. Never rush the swing; always keep it controlled.

Side bends

The waist, abdomen, and lower back link the actions of the upper and lower body. You must make sure that the muscles in these areas are properly stretched because you will use them in all track and field events.

1 Bend to one side from the hips. Keep your body facing forward and your hips straight. Hold the stretch for 10 seconds. Do not bounce.

2 Raise your body back into the upright position and rest for a couple of seconds.

Try to bring your hands together above your head; if you find this too difficult, rest one hand on your thigh instead.

3 Now bend over to the other side, making sure your body is still facing forward. Keep breathing normally. Next time, try to stretch a little farther.

Keep your body facing forward during this exercise.

Your legs should be slightly bent.

Feet should be shoulder-width apart.

Hamstring stretch

One of the most common athletic injuries is a pulled or torn hamstring. This exercise, in which a friend applies gentle pressure to your back, allows you to stretch your hamstring farther than you could on your own.

Press gently so as not to cause strain on the lower back.

With your arms outstretched, relax your body down over your legs and hold your ankles or toes.

Inner thigh stretch

Strains in the inner thigh and the groin area are usually caused by sudden movements. Stretching reduces the chance of this happening by ensuring that the muscle is flexible enough to cope with any changes in length.

Try to keep your shoulders level.

Keep your body upright and facing forward.

Rest your hands on your legs for balance.

Bend your leg at right angles to your knee with your foot facing forward.

Controlled movements
Do all the exercises in your warm-up slowly, making sure that your movements are smooth and controlled.

Hold your head in line with your body.

To increase the stretch, lower your hips toward the ground slowly.

Keep this leg straight during the stretch, with your foot facing forward.

Your toes should be in line with your bent knee.

Quadriceps stretch

Stretch your quadriceps, or thigh muscle, by pulling back your knee so that your heel touches your buttocks. Balance by placing your arm against a wall, a friend's shoulder, or some equipment.

Use this arm for balance.

Don't lock this leg because this will put too much strain on your knee.

Calf muscle stretch

Stand about 12 in (30 cm) from a wall and lean forward onto it. Bend one knee and stretch your other leg backward. Try to keep your heel on the ground and feel the stretch in your lower leg.

Keep this heel pressed into the ground.

Push your hips forward.

Sprint drills

T HE SPRINTING EVENTS – the 100 m, the 200 m, and the 400 m – are probably the most popular track and field events. Sprinting requires short, fast explosions of power and the most successful sprinters can combine speed with quick reactions and tremendous stamina. Exercises called sprint drills help improve these sprinting techniques.

Heel flicks

This drill is designed to make your legs move faster by improving the speed with which your heel comes up to your buttocks. It also strengthens your hamstrings (the muscles running down the backs of your legs).

1 Hold your body upright, look straight ahead, and start jogging using very short strides.

Loosely cup your hands.

Don't let your knee swing forward.

2 With each step, pull your heel up sharply so that it makes contact with your buttocks.

Pull your elbows back.

Keep your hips high.

Fold this leg up behind you.

High knee lifts

One of the most important techniques in sprinting is the high knee lift. This very powerful movement helps increase the length of your stride, which in turn makes you go faster. The high knee lift is produced by the hips and the thigh muscles. Events such as throwing the javelin, jumping, and hurdling will also benefit from this drill.

1 Begin by walking or jogging on the balls of your feet. Concentrate on the movements in this drill; think about what the best sprinters look like when they are sprinting toward the finish line.

Practicing drills
All of the drills shown here can be done on the spot or while jogging. Each one is practiced over a fixed distance or for a fixed number of times.

2 Bring your knees up to hip height with each stride. Pump your arms backward and forward from your hips to your shoulders.

Relax your jaw and keep your chin up.

Try to keep your foot flexed during this drill.

Keep your shoulders back; if you lean forward it's harder to lift your knees.

Look straight ahead.

Make sure you stay up on the balls of your feet as if you were sprinting.

Ankle rolls

Sprinting is done mostly on the balls of the feet. Ankle rolls help loosen your ankles and increase their range of movement. This in turn enables you to stay up on the balls of your feet during sprints. Middle- and long-distance running also benefit from this drill.

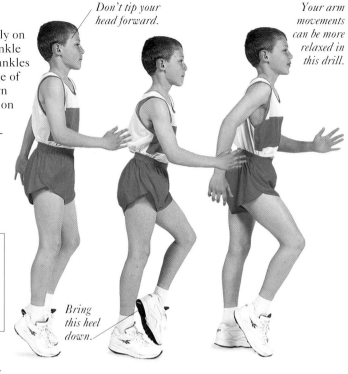

Don't tip your head forward.

Your arm movements can be more relaxed in this drill.

Bring this heel down.

Feet positions
Keep your feet moving along the ground during this drill, but make sure they are never more than a few inches apart.

1 Roll right up onto the balls of your feet.

2 Step forward slightly and bring your heel down.

3 Repeat the drill using your other foot.

Track officials

"On your marks ..... set ..... bang!" As the starter fires his gun, the race begins. The starter has to ensure that all the runners begin at the same time. If any of the runners "false starts" (leaves the starting block before the command), a marksman fires a gun to bring them back to their starting positions. A runner is allowed two false starts before being disqualified from a race. Other race officials include timekeepers and the chief track judge.

3 Repeat the movement using your other leg. Don't let your hips drop during this drill; it is a sign of bad technique.

Keep moving your arms.

Your knee should be at the same height as your hips.

4 High knee lifts can be very tiring at first. Allow yourself a minute or two to recover before you repeat this drill.

Standing start

Middle- and long-distance races use a standing start, which has just one starting command. When you hear "On your marks," place most of your weight on your front foot and lean forward in a comfortable position, ready to sprint off on the Bang! of the starter's gun. For those who have not yet learned to use starting blocks (see page 12), this type of start can also be used for sprinting events.

Behind the line
The marksman checks that your feet are behind the line before the race starts.

Starting the race

IN THE EARLY DAYS of track and field, sprinters used to dig small holes in the ground to give them something to push off against at the start of a race. Today, runners in the 100 m, the 200 m, and the 400 m use starting blocks to provide a more solid base to push against. The blocks must be fastened to the track and are fitted with tiny spikes along their edges to ensure they do not damage the track surface.

The starting block

A starting block consists of a metal bar with a pair of adjustable foot pads attached to it. The blocks can be connected to a device that detects if a foot has left the block before the starting gun fires to within 0.1 seconds. This is used to decide if any runner false starts (see page 11).

The foot pads can be moved and their angle adjusted.

Holes for adjusting foot pad

The hand position

In the "On your marks" position, your hands must be behind the starting line. Use your fingers and thumb to form a bridge; do not lay your palms on the track.

Preparing to run

An athlete's state of mind before a race is as important as his physical condition. Linford Christie, above, is famous for his "tunnel vision" concentration, in which he focuses his mind totally on the race ahead.

On your marks ...

1 When you hear the command "On your marks," position your hands behind the lines and place your feet on the blocks. The front block should be about 10–12 in (30–40 cm) behind the starting line; the other block is the length of your foot behind this.

Be comfortable
You should feel comfortable in the blocks. Experiment until you find the position that suits you best.

2 On "Set," raise your hips and tilt your body forward so that your shoulders are in line with your arms. Press both feet hard against the blocks ready to drive out.

To get a good push off the blocks, keep your legs bent.

Your hips should be higher than your shoulders.

Your front knee should be in line with your arms.

The rear block should form a right angle with the ground.

If you are not strong enough to take your weight on your fingers, try resting on your knuckles instead.

Running the bend

In the 200 m, the 400 m, and the 4 x 100 m relay, you must stay in your own lane as you run the bend. Because you approach the bend at top speed, you will find that you are pushed to the outside of your lane. To avoid this, take shorter strides and lean into the bend. Try to run close to the inside of your lane because this will reduce the distance you have to run.

Keep looking ahead; don't look around at the other runners.

Pull your arms back.

Drop your inside arm to help you lean into the bend.

Take shorter strides.

Sprinting to victory

This picture of Frank Fredericks of Namibia was taken at the 1993 World Championships in Stuttgart, Germany. As he approaches the bend on the 200 m, Fredericks's body twists slightly as he drops his left shoulder and leans into the bend. This helps him keep his legs moving smoothly as he runs the bend. Fredericks won this race.

The finish

A well-timed dip finish can make all the difference to your position in a race. The winner is the person whose torso, or trunk, crosses the finishing line first. About three strides from the line, pull your arms back and thrust your chest and shoulders forward as you push yourself, or "dip," across the line. Try not to dip too soon however; this will slow you down because you stop pumping your arms.

3 At the sound of the starter's gun, push back hard against the blocks. Take your hands off the ground as you drive your body forward.

Leaving the block
Try to run out of the blocks with a smooth, continuous action.

Keep your head and body low to improve your acceleration.

Your hands leave the ground as you push off against the block.

Bring this leg forward to form your first stride.

Pump your arms backward and forward quickly.

Keep looking down at the track; if you raise your head, your hips will drop.

Push your front leg back against the block.

4 As you push hard off the front block, swing your back leg forward into the first stride. Keep your body low until you reach your top speed and your natural stride length.

Your arms should be supporting most of your weight.

Different starts
In the 200 m, the 400 m, and the 800 m, the start is staggered to ensure the athletes run the same distance.

Training for longer distances

T HE MAIN MIDDLE- AND LONG-
distance events are the 800 m, the 1500 m,
the 3000 m, the 5000 m, and the 10,000 m.
Runners in these events must be able to run
at a steady pace over long distances, and need
a slow, constant supply of energy. Training or
conditioning programs help you build up the
stamina and the muscle strength that you need
to compete successfully in these races.

*Try not to lock
your arms or dip
your body too low.*

*Keep your
feet apart
for balance.*

*Keep your
stomach
pulled in.*

*Don't arch
your back.*

Push-ups

Support your weight with your hands beneath your shoulders.
Keep your body in a straight line and bend your arms to bring
your nose down to the ground. If you find a full push-up too
difficult, try putting some of your weight on your knees. As you
become stronger, gradually move your knees off the ground.

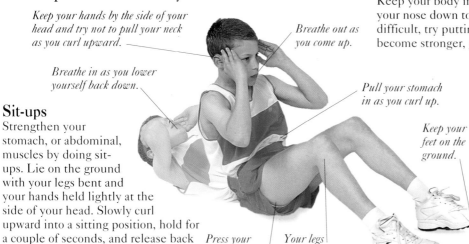

*Keep your hands by the side of your
head and try not to pull your neck
as you curl upward.*

*Breathe out as
you come up.*

*Breathe in as you lower
yourself back down.*

*Pull your stomach
in as you curl up.*

*Keep your
feet on the
ground.*

Sit-ups

Strengthen your
stomach, or abdominal,
muscles by doing sit-
ups. Lie on the ground
with your legs bent and
your hands held lightly at the
side of your head. Slowly curl
upward into a sitting position, hold for
a couple of seconds, and release back
down. Repeat the exercise, keeping
your legs bent throughout.

*Press your
lower back to
the floor.*

*Your legs
should be bent
all the time.*

*If this position is uncomfortable,
bring your feet in closer to your
body.*

The curl

You could start with this easier version
of the sit-up. With your feet apart, curl
your body up and reach for your knees.

The jump squat

Sprinters and middle- and long-distance
runners need very strong leg muscles. This
exercise works in two ways. Squatting
strengthens the muscles that run in
your thighs – the hamstrings at the
back and the quadriceps at the
front – while jumping increases
your stamina.

2 Bend your knees
and push your body
downward. Keep your
back straight and try
not to lean forward.

*Keep your head
up and look
straight ahead.*

*Keep your
back straight.*

1 Start with your feet
shoulder-width apart
and place your hands
on your hips. You
should also finish in
this position.

*Your legs should
be straight as
you jump up.*

Repetitions
As you become stronger,
increase the number of times you
repeat each exercise.

*Point your toes
downward.*

3 Leap up into the air
quickly. Try to go as
high as you can.

Using a medicine ball

A medicine ball is a weighted leather or rubber ball. When you do exercises that involve a medicine ball, the ball provides resistance for you to work against. This is one of the best ways of improving your strength and speed.

1 Sit on the floor and ask a friend or your coach to gently throw a medicine ball to you. Lean back slightly as you catch the ball and make sure you keep your stomach pulled in.

Bring the ball into your chest as you catch it.

Keep pulling in your stomach.

2 Throw the medicine ball back to your partner. Use both hands and push your arms away from your chest. Rest for a couple of seconds and then repeat the exercise. Make sure you aim the ball accurately to avoid accidents.

Straighten your arms as you return the ball.

Raise your body into a sitting position.

Keep your legs bent.

Try to keep your feet on the ground.

Hamstring flicks

Try to make sure that you flick your legs at just the right moment during this exercise, otherwise your hamstrings will not benefit properly from the move.

1 Lie on the floor and ask a friend to roll a medicine ball down your back and your legs.

2 When the ball touches your heels, flick it upward to your partner.

Make sure you roll the ball carefully.

Flick the ball with your heels.

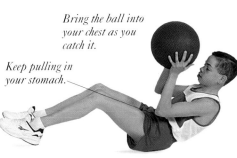

Kick-outs

1 Lie on the floor with your arms by your sides. Raise your legs off the ground and ask a friend to throw a ball at your feet.

Straighten your legs.

Support your weight with your arms.

2 With the soles of your feet together, kick the ball back to your partner.

Bring your knees in to your chest when you kick the ball.

Press your back to the ground.

Hill running

This is an excellent way to strengthen your leg muscles and improve your stamina. Shorten your stride and practice running quickly up short hills or slowly up longer hills.

Cross-country

Include cross-country races in your training program. These are usually run over about 3.2 miles (5 km), and often involve obstacles such as hills, streams, gates, and thick mud. Cross-country runs are excellent for building strength and stamina.

Fun run

As their name suggests, fun runs are non-competitive races that are often held to benefit charities. Because they are not officially classed as races, there are no restrictions on age or distance, and participants range from experienced athletes using the race to improve their technique and stamina, to complete beginners running to raise funds for charity.

Race walking

Race walkers adapt the way they walk by rotating their hips to produce a faster, longer stride. Their feet must make continuous contact with the ground. Training improves the range of movement in the hips, and so can help you in hurdles (see pages 18–19).

The relay

ONE OF THE MOST EXCITING track and field events is the relay. It is often the highlight of major competitions and is usually the last event held. Unlike most track and field events, the relay is a team event in which four runners each run a section, or leg, of the total distance. Each team member is picked for a particular strength. The fastest runner runs first, the strongest runners run second and last, and the best bend runner runs third. A tube called a baton is passed from the first runner to the second, and so on. The main relay events are the 4 x 100 m and the 4 x 400 m.

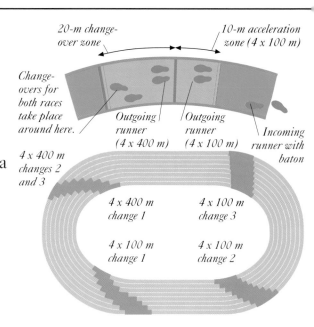

20-m change-over zone

10-m acceleration zone (4 x 100 m)

Change-overs for both races take place around here.

Outgoing runner (4 x 400 m)

Outgoing runner (4 x 100 m)

Incoming runner with baton

4 x 400 m changes 2 and 3

4 x 400 m change 1

4 x 100 m change 3

4 x 100 m change 1

4 x 100 m change 2

The baton

A relay baton is a smooth, hollow tube about 12 in (30 cm) long and 5 in (12 cm) around. It can be made of wood, metal, or plastic and weighs only about 2 oz (50 grams). The batons are usually brightly colored to make them easier to see.

The changeover zone

The baton changeover must take place within a specific 20-m area called the changeover zone. In the 4 x 100-m relay, this area is marked on the track in yellow; in the 4 x 400 m, it is marked in blue. If the changeover does not occur within this specified area, the team will be disqualified.

The changeover

A good changeover can save valuable seconds in a race. During training, practice handing over the baton to the teammate you will be running with. In both relays, the changeover should take place in the last 10 m of the zone, when both runners are running at the same speed. In the 4 x 100 m, the outgoing runner does not look back to receive the baton, but in the 4 x 400 m, which is very tiring, the outgoing runner looks back when the baton is passed.

Teamwork

I am the incoming runner in this race and am using the downsweep pass (see above right) to pass the baton to my teammate Linford Christie.

The runners in this sequence are using the upsweep pass (see page 17).

1 As you sprint into the changeover zone, call out "hand" or "stick" to your teammate, who then stretches back her hand to receive the baton.

Bring the baton upward.

Keep pumping this arm backward and forward.

As the incoming runner, it is your responsibility to make sure that the baton is passed safely.

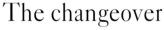

The upsweep pass

Of the two relay passes, the upsweep pass is easier to learn and safer to use. The outgoing runner holds her arm low, which makes it easier for the incoming runner to place the baton in her hand.

1 When she hears a shout from the incoming runner, the outgoing runner stretches out her right hand, palm downward. Her thumb and index finger should form a "V" shape.

Fingers and thumb form a "V" shape.

2 The incoming runner brings the baton up into the "V" of the outgoing runner's hand. Runner 1 should hold the first quarter of the baton, runner 2 the second quarter, and so on.

The runners' hands are very close in this pass.

3 The incoming runner lets go of the baton when she sees that the outgoing runner has grasped it. The baton is carried in the outgoing runner's right hand, and transferred to the next runner's left hand.

2 You should now both be running at the same speed. Bring the baton upward and place it into the "V" shape formed by your teammate's outstretched hand.

Planning tactics
In training, figure out where the incoming runner should be when the outgoing runner starts to run. This point is called the check mark, and you can mark it on the track.

The downsweep pass

When it is done properly, the downsweep pass is the quicker of the two relay passes. However, it is a more difficult pass because the outgoing runner holds her arm higher to receive the baton.

1 The incoming runner grips the end of the baton, while the outgoing runner pushes her right hand back, palm upward.

Your palm should face upward.

2 The incoming runner passes the baton downward into the outstretched palm. The outgoing runner should form a "V" shape with her fingers and thumb.

Bring the baton downward. *Keep your fingers together.*

3 The outgoing runner takes the baton in her right hand, ready to pass it into the next runner's left hand.

Make sure you grasp the baton firmly.

3 With the baton safely in her hand, your teammate sprints off. You can start to slow down, but should not leave your lane until all the other runners have passed by.

Keep the baton in your right hand, ready to pass it into the next runner's left hand.

Don't look back as you reach back to receive the baton.

If you drop the baton, you, not your teammate, must pick it up. You can leave your lane to do this.

Keep running at full speed until you have passed on the baton.

Hurdles

IN THE 1896 OLYMPICS, the first hurdles race was run over a distance of 100 m. The hurdles used were actually sheep barriers, nailed to the track. The barriers were extremely heavy and could seriously injure an athlete who knocked one over. Today, the main hurdling events are the 100 m (for women), the 110 m (for men), and the 400 m (for both). Modern hurdles consist of a wooden bar supported by two adjustable metal stands. They are not fixed to the track, but are weighted so that it takes a force of at least 8 lb (3.6 kg) to knock one over.

Looking ahead
In addition to being physically demanding, hurdles also require tremendous concentration. As you clear each hurdle, keep your head up and your eyes focused on the hurdle ahead, ready to sprint toward it.

Hurdle heights
The height of a hurdle varies according to the age and sex of the athletes in the race. Under 14 (U-14) boys and U-17 girls use a 30-in (76-cm) hurdle; U-15 boys, U-20 girls, and senior women use a 34-in (84-cm) hurdle; U-17 boys use a 36-in (91.4-cm) hurdle, and senior men use a 42-in (106.7-cm) hurdle.

As you approach the hurdle, lift up your lead leg and bend your knee.

Drive forward with your arms.

Lead leg

Trail leg

Drive yourself off the ground with your trail leg.

Straighten your lead leg so that your heel drives over the hurdle.

Use this arm for balance.

Try to turn your foot outward to avoid knocking the hurdle over.

Bend your trail leg as your lead leg starts to cross the hurdle.

Hurdling technique
When you are hurdling, try to develop a smooth, continuous sprinting action that is only slightly interrupted when you jump over each hurdle. Figure out the number of strides between the start of the race and the first hurdle so that you take off at the right spot with the correct leg (usually called the lead leg). This will help you achieve a good hurdling rhythm and will also help you determine the number of strides to take between the rest of the hurdles.

Hurdles training

Like a sprinter (see pages 10/11), a hurdler needs to be fast and strong. However, hurdlers also need to work on increasing the range of movement in their hips and on their technique for clearing the hurdle. In this exercise, stand close to the side of a hurdle and ask a partner to support you as you practice bringing your trail leg over the hurdle.

Grip your partner's wrists for balance.

Your partner should bend his arms slightly as you come forward.

Come forward with your trail leg and drive your knee over the hurdle.

Point your toes outward.

Watch your trail leg
This exercise is especially important because you can be disqualified if you let your leg trail around the outside of a hurdle.

Your trail leg should be about 24 in (60 cm) behind your lead leg.

Keep your knee high, as if you were about to sprint off.

Hamstring stretch

Try this stretch to really loosen your hamstrings – the main muscles used in hurdling. Place your leg on top of a hurdle and bend forward to bring your chest onto your knee.

Keep this knee slightly bent.

Hold on to your ankle as you lower your chest onto your knee.

Try to keep your body as upright as possible; this will help you clear the hurdle.

Pull your right arm back.

As you land, pull your right arm back so that your trail leg is pulled over the hurdle.

Sprint away from the hurdle in an upright position.

As you clear the hurdle, pull your trail leg up sharply. Try to keep your heel close to your buttocks.

Knocking over a hurdle
You will not be disqualified if you accidentally knock over a hurdle during a race, but it will throw you off balance and could slow you down.

Bring your lead leg back onto the track quickly because you lose speed while you are in the air.

Try to land on the ball of your foot.

Triple jump

THE TRIPLE JUMP is the one of the most complex and demanding jumping events. Its origins can be traced back as far as the ancient Greek Olympics, when there were no set rules and jumpers could use two hops and a jump or three steps and a jump. Even in the first modern Olympics, the winner, James Conolly, won with two hops and a jump. Today, the rules dictate that jumpers must take a "hop, step, and jump," while trying to cover the greatest possible distance. As a triple jumper, you need to be springy, with very strong legs. Rhythm is also important because you need to make the flight times of each stage as equal as possible and should be able to sense the TAA–TAA–TAA timing when you land.

Groin stretch

This stretch helps loosen some of the muscles that you use during the hop and step flights. Turn to the side and take a large step forward with your right leg. Bend your knee, making sure that you keep it directly above your ankle. Extend your left leg with your heel off the ground and feel the stretch in your upper thigh and groin as you lower your hips toward the ground. Repeat using your other leg.

Keep your back leg straight.

Don't let your knee go over your toes.

Keep your heel off the ground.

Hop, step ...

1 Try to build up speed on the approach run to make up for the speed and distance you lose each time you take off. Limit the number of strides you take to your age. For example, if you are 11 years old, take 11 strides, if you are 12, take 12, and so on until you reach the age of 17.

During each stage of the triple jump, make sure that your trail leg does not touch the ground before the final landing or you will be disqualified.

Levels of effort
Try to distribute the amount of effort that you put into each phase as follows: 37% (hop) – 26% (step) – 37% (jump).

Pump your arms hard until you take off for the hop.

When you swing one arm forward and one arm backward, it is known as a single arm shift.

2 Your hop takeoff should be quick and "active." Strike the takeoff board with a flat foot and drive your takeoff leg forward and upward so that your thigh is parallel with the runway.

Swing your right knee forward powerfully.

Bring your right leg back.

Bring your foot down and back slightly to maintain your speed. Try to hit the takeoff board with a flat foot.

Extend this leg fully so that you take off at an angle of about 15–18°.

3 Swing your left leg through into a horizontal position so that it is parallel with the ground and drive your right knee back. Just as you are about to land, reach out with your left foot and "claw" the ground backward to pull your body forward.

Inner thigh stretch

This stretch increases your flexibility and can help you avoid injury if you land awkwardly during one of the stages. With your legs apart, bend your right knee and feel the stretch in the inner thigh of your left leg as you lower your hips. Hold the position for a count of ten and then repeat on the other side.

Look straight ahead and keep your body upright.

Rest your hands on your thighs for balance.

Face forward.

Rest your hands lightly on the top of your thigh for balance.

This foot should be flat on the floor and pointing in the same direction as your body.

Your foot should be directly below your knee and face forward.

Turn your foot forward to increase the stretch.

Hold your head high to stop yourself from tipping forward.

4 When you land, your foot should be slightly ahead of your knees and hips. Your body is pulled forward by the clawing action of your landing foot and by swinging your right knee through.

Keep your body upright throughout each of the stages.

Bring your left leg through into a horizontal position.

Try to feel the TAA–TAA–TAA rhythm each time you land.

The angle of the step takeoff is about 13–15°, which is lower than the angle of the hop takeoff.

As you prepare to land, reach out with your left leg to "claw" the ground.

Try to keep your thigh parallel with the ground as your foot reaches out to land.

Swing your right knee through.

Try to land with a flat foot. Bend your knees as little as possible.

5 Still using a single arm swinging action, go into the step phase. The flight looks similar to that of the hop. With your legs wide apart, push your right leg upward and drive it forward.

Jump over onto the next page ...

Long jump

O F ALL THE jumping events, the long jump is perhaps the most natural to perform and the easiest to learn. The goal is to take off from behind a specific line and try to cover the longest distance possible before landing in a sand-filled pit. The event is made harder by the tremendous speeds that long jumpers have to reach in their approach run, because this directly affects the length of their jump. The most successful long jumpers are often built like sprinters – tall, with long legs and good explosive power. In training, they also try to develop strength, a good sense of rhythm, and the ability to judge distances accurately.

Long jump

There are four distinct stages in the long jump: the approach run, the takeoff, the flight, and the landing. You should hit the takeoff board at maximum speed, so practice pacing your approach run to get the best possible start to your jump.

1 Strike the takeoff board with the whole of your foot and then quickly drive your free leg upward and forward. Extend your other leg and keep your body upright as you push off.

Keep your hips high.

Extend this leg.

Drive your free leg up and forward.

... and jump

6 The step landing is the hardest of the three triple jump landings because it is done on your weakest leg and because you have lost a lot of your speed and momentum on the previous two takeoffs. As you land, swing your arms forward to prepare for your next takeoff.

If you take off past the strip, your jump will be declared a "no jump."

Strip of modeling clay or damp sand

Taking off

The wooden takeoff board is about 6 in (20 cm) wide. It is embedded in the runway and is painted white so that it can be clearly seen. At the edge of the board is a strip of modeling clay or damp sand. If you make a mark in this strip, your jump will be a "no jump."

Bring your arms up together as you take off for the jump. This swinging action is a double arm shift.

Swing your free leg forward to increase your momentum.

7 Drive off immediately with your landing leg. The jump takeoff is higher than those of the hop and the step, and has an angle of about 20–24°.

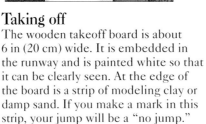

Move your arms at the same time as your legs.

Move your legs in a cycling action as you travel through the air.

2 During the flight, try to take one or two strides with your legs. This action is called the hitch kick, and it helps to propel your body forward through the air.

3 As you prepare to land, bring your legs together and swing them out in front of your body. Keep your feet high and swing your arms back as your body comes forward.

Swing your arms back.

Straighten your legs ahead of you.

Your approach run
As in the triple jump, calculate the number of strides in your approach run according to your age.

4 Once your feet hit the sand, bend your knees slightly and try to pull yourself past the mark your feet have made.

Throw your arms forward over your head.

Pull your body forward so that you don't sit back in the sand.

Bend your knees as you land.

8 As you bring your right knee through to meet your left knee, you appear to hang in the air momentarily until you fold your body forward, ready to land. This movement is known as a "hang jump."

Swing your arms and body forward to stop yourself from falling back when you straighten your legs.

Straighten your legs as you fold your body.

Keep your feet high so that they stay clear of the sand.

Measuring distances
Both the triple jump and the long jump are measured from the takeoff board to the nearest mark in the sand. You should therefore always try to fall forward when you land and walk out of the front of the pit. If you fall or walk backward, your jump will be measured from that shorter distance.

Takeoff board   *Buttock imprint*   *Hand imprint*   *Foot imprint*

Bring your arms forward and down toward the ground; this will pull your body over your feet.

9 As you hit the sand, throw your arms forward and let your knees bend slightly. This will stop your body from falling backward when you land (see above).

Let your knees bend as you land; this will propel your body forward past your footprints in the sand.

High jump

ONE OF THE MOST important factors in the high jump is the equipment that the athletes have to land on. Up until the early 1960s, high jumpers had to land on sand, and were therefore forced to use a jumping technique that guaranteed a safe landing. The introduction of foam landing areas enabled athletes to concentrate on clearing the bar. Like the long and triple jumps, the high jump has four stages: the approach run, the takeoff, clearing the bar, and landing.

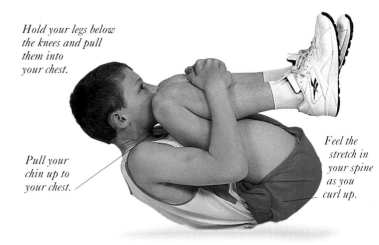

Hold your legs below the knees and pull them into your chest.

Pull your chin up to your chest.

Feel the stretch in your spine as you curl up.

The curl

The Fosbury flop technique puts a lot of strain and pressure on your back. This exercise stretches the muscles in your back and helps prevent injuries while you are jumping. Lie flat on the floor and pull your knees in to your chest so that your body curls upward.

The Fosbury flop

The two main high jump techniques are the Fosbury flop and the scissors (see page 25). The flop was first used by American athlete Dick Fosbury at the 1968 Olympics in Mexico. Instead of performing the usual straddle or scissors jump (see above right), Fosbury stunned the crowd by "flopping" over the bar backward and landing on his back. Although this technique is slightly harder to learn than the scissors jump, it does allow you to jump much higher.

The approach for the Fosbury flop is "J"-shaped; straight at the beginning and slightly curved at the end.

1 Your approach run should consist of about 8–10 strides. The first 4–5 strides are straight, and allow you to build up speed, while the second 4–5 are curved to bring you up to the bar.

Keep the shoulder nearest to the bar as high as possible.

Lean away from the bar on your approach run.

2 As you approach the bar, make your last strides shorter and quicker. Try to land on your heels, as this will allow you to lower your hips and bend your takeoff leg, ready to jump.

Bend your takeoff leg as you prepare to jump.

3 Your takeoff foot should now be pointing in the direction you want to go. Keep your inside leg bent as you thrust your thigh upward and forward.

Raise this arm as you take off.

Keep your inside leg bent.

Point your toes in the direction that you are jumping.

Scoring
You are allowed to attempt each jump three times. However, you will be disqualified after three consecutive failures, even if they are at different heights.

Back arch

For this exercise, in which you loosen up the muscles in your back, lie on the floor and place your hands under your shoulders. Keep your hips on the ground and push up slowly with your arms until your upper body is in an upright position. Hold the stretch for a count of ten, lower your body back to the starting position, and then repeat.

Don't let your head tilt back.

Raise your body into an upright position.

Try to keep your hips on the ground and bend from your waist.

Keep your toes tucked under.

Try not to lock your elbows as you straighten your arms.

This picture shows a bent leg scissors jump.

Swing your inside leg upward and over the bar. Your body should be in a sitting position.

Take off from your outside foot.

The scissors jump

Before the introduction of a foam landing area, the scissors jump was the only high jump technique that guaranteed a safe landing in the sand pit. The scissors jump is also the one that many beginners learn first because it helps them develop a good takeoff technique.

4 As a result of the curved approach run, your body turns as you jump, and is propelled head first over the bar.

Pull your legs clear of the bar.

5 As you clear the bar, lift your head and shoulders to look at your feet. Keep your back straight and press your shoulders back and your heels in. This will prevent your hips from dropping and lift your legs up over the bar. Try to land on your back and shoulders.

Jump upward, rather than toward the bar.

Aim to jump over the middle of the bar, which is the lowest part.

Discus

THE DISCUS DATES BACK to the 8th century BC. The ancient Greek poet Homer makes several references to it throughout his work, and the famous bronze statue by the sculptor Myron (480–440 BC), the "*Discobolos*," depicts a discus thrower. The event involves an athlete rotating around a circle before releasing a flat, disklike object called a discus. Up until 1912, the discus was thrown from an angled platform. Today, athletes have to throw from within a circle 8.2 ft (2.5 m) in diameter. They must make one and a half turns of the circle before they release the discus. This means that the action is more of a slinging one than a throw.

Straighten your back arm as you swing to stretch your shoulder and chest muscles.

Look over your shoulder at your outstretched arm.

Loosening up
Prepare for the twisting, swinging action of the discus with this exercise. Stand with your feet hip-width apart and swing your arms from side to side. Twist from your waist and try to keep your hips facing forward as you swing.

Keep your hips facing foward throughout.

Bend your knees slightly.

Rest the edge of the discus on the inside of your wrist.

Spread your fingers out evenly and tuck the tips under the discus.

The equipment
The discus is made of wood and is surrounded by a metal rim. The center piece can be made from wood, metal, or rubber.

Safety
Because the discus is released after a turn, the throw must take place from inside a "cage" to avoid accidents.

The grip
Hold the discus loosely in the palm of your throwing hand with the rim resting on your fingertips. Your fingers can be spread out evenly (right), or you can keep your first two fingers together (left). In both grips, use your thumb to keep the discus firmly in position.

The standing throw
One of the best ways to learn how to throw the discus is to begin with a standing start. This will teach you the basics of the event and will also help with your future training. Using this technique, gradually build up your speed by swinging your arms and your body from your hips.

The palm of your hand should face downward.

1 Stand with your feet hip-width apart and hold the discus in whichever hand feels most comfortable. Turn your body slightly as you extend your arm backward.

Hands and feet
The feet positions shown here are for a right-handed thrower. If you are left-handed, use the opposite feet.

Start with your weight on your right foot.

Pull your body and shoulder through by swinging your hips.

2 Swing the discus forward, turning your body forward as you do so. Bring your opposite hand up to meet the discus during these practice throws if you are worried about dropping it.

The turn

Once you have mastered the swinging action, try turning as you throw. Start from the back of the circle and stand with your legs bent and slightly apart and your arms wide.

Shift your weight onto the foot opposite your throwing arm and pivot around on this foot. Swing your body around and land on your other foot.

As you turn to the back of the circle for the second time, start to straighten your body and bring your throwing arm forward in a wide, swinging action.

Release the discus and bring your right arm across your body and your right foot forward to stop you from falling over.

Briefly support the discus at the top of your swing, before bringing it back down for the next swing.

Try to swing your shoulder and your throwing arm slightly farther with each rotation.

Bend your knees slightly lower with your next swing.

With your weight on your right leg, pivot on your left foot.

The release
Al Oerter, an American Olympic gold medalist, is seen here releasing the discus. He presses down on the leading edge of the discus so that it flies off at the correct angle.

Transfer your weight onto your left foot and lift your right heel off the ground.

3 Bring the discus up to the top of your swing. Your weight should now be on your left foot. Turn this foot to face the direction of your throw. This is the position you should be in just before you release the discus.

4 Go back to your starting position and repeat the sequence. Bend your knees as you rotate your body and gradually build up your speed and momentum.

1 *Start with your feet apart, facing 12 o'clock.*

2 *Swing your right foot around to face 6 o'clock.*

3 *Bring your left foot around to face 6 o'clock.*

4 *With both feet facing 6 o'clock, you are ready to throw.*

The follow-through
As the discus flies off Oerter's index finger, he steps forward onto his right foot and lifts his left foot off the ground. This helps him keep his balance and stay within the throwing circle.

Leaving the circle
Once you have completed your throw, make sure that you leave the turning circle from the back, or you will be disqualified.

Foot positions
The position of your feet when throwing the discus is crucial. In the diagram above, the circle has been divided up like a clock face to make the instructions easier to understand.

Javelin

U NLIKE THE OTHER throwing events, the javelin takes place from a runway rather than from within a throwing circle. The event has developed from the spears thrown by our ancestors during hunting and warfare, but the distances thrown today are far greater than they could ever have imagined. This is the result of improvements in javelin design and technique. In fact, in 1984 the javelin had to be redesigned because it was actually flying over the infield and onto the track – a distance of over 330 ft (100 m)!

The grip

The two main javelin grips are shown right. The middle finger grip (top), in which you grip the javelin with your middle finger and thumb, is the more natural of the two grips. In the "V" grip (bottom), the javelin rests between your first two fingers. This makes it easier to grip, but is often uncomfortable.

Middle finger grip

"V" grip

1 Try to build up speed on your approach run. Hold the javelin high with your palm facing upward. This will help you achieve the best result and avoid injury.

2 In the last strides of your approach run, stretch your throwing arm back so that the javelin is behind you. You should also drive your right knee high up into your last stride. This is called a crossover stride.

Cord grip

The equipment

The javelin has a wooden or metal shaft, with a pointed metal head and a cord hand grip.

Shaft Head

Shot put

P UTTING THE WEIGHT, as the shot was first called, originated at the Scottish Highland Games, possibly around the 14th century. The weights used were large stones that were too heavy to be thrown, but that could be pushed one-handed from the shoulder. Today, a heavy metal ball called a shot is used instead of a stone, but the technique remains the same.

The equipment

The shot is a solid brass or iron ball. Its weight varies from 3.25 kg for U13 girls to 7.26 kg for men and 4 kg for women.

Holding the shot

Rest the shot at the base of three of the fingers on your throwing, or putting, hand. Use your thumb and little finger to hold it steady. The shot should remain tucked under your chin until just before you release it and should not touch your palm at any time. Remember the rule that "all shot putters should have a clean palm and a dirty neck"!

Putting technique

In the "linear," or "O'Brien," technique, you lean out over the back of the circle and then move across it, pushing the shot outward and upward from your shoulder. With the rotational technique, you spin within the circle to build up momentum before releasing the shot.

Extend this arm to help you balance.

Keep your elbow high throughout the sequence.

1 Stand with your feet about 24 in (60 cm) apart. Tuck the shot under your chin, keeping the elbow of your putting arm high.

2 Bring your feet together as you skip or shuffle to your left.

This "moving throw" is an easier version of the "linear," or "O'Brien," technique.

3 If you throw with your right hand, you will land on your right foot as a result of the crossover stride, with your body leaning back and your hips pushed forward. Hold the javelin high and behind your body.

🏃 **Scoring**
The javelin must land point first for your throw to be valid. The throw will be measured from the first mark the javelin makes.

4 Drive your left leg forward to complete your last stride, leaving your right arm and the javelin behind your body. Bend your right leg slightly to drive your hips forward. This will give your body a slightly arched shape. Swing your left arm outward to help you balance.

5 Whip your chest and shoulders forward as you bring your throwing arm through to release the javelin. Make sure you keep your elbow high throughout the release. This makes the javelin go high above your shoulder and head, and helps avoid injuries to your elbow joint.

6 After you have released the javelin, your right leg will continue to come forward into your next stride. Bend your leg to slow you down and to stop you from going forward over the scratch line. You must remain behind this line until your throw has been measured, or it will be declared invalid.

---

3 Place your weight on your right foot when you land and bring your left leg forward. Bend your knees, ready to push the shot away from your shoulder.

4 Swing your right hip around to bring your body forward. Push the shot out from under your chin.

🏃 **Scoring**
The shot must land within a clearly marked 40° sector for your throw to be valid.

Flick the shot off your fingertips.

5 Try to push the shot upward and forward from your chin as quickly as possible. The higher and faster you release the shot, the farther it will travel.

6 To follow through after the release, bring your right leg forward and bend it to prevent yourself from going over the wooden stopboard at the front of the circle.

Use your shoulder to drive the shot upward.

Swing your right hip around as you prepare to throw.

Straighten your body.

Bend your knees.

Lift your left foot off the ground as you follow through.

Combined events

T HE DECATHLON and the heptathlon are designed to find the best all-around male and female athletes. The decathlon is for men and consists of 10 events. The first modern decathlon was held in Germany in 1911, and all the events took place on the same day. It appeared in the Olympics in 1912 and, like today's event, was held over two days. The heptathlon, which is for women and consists of seven events, is also held over two days. It was introduced in 1981 to replace the pentathlon, which had five events. The javelin and the 800 m were added, putting the emphasis on strength as well as speed. The winner in each combined event is decided by a scoring system in which competitors win points for the time, distance, and speed achieved in each event. The athlete with the highest score wins.

Day one

The athlete shown in this sequence is Jackie Joyner Kersee of the United States, one of the top heptathletes.

1. 100-m hurdles
The events in the heptathlon are carried out in the order shown here. There should be a 30 minute break between each event. The combined events test an athlete's speed, strength, agility, and endurance. Speed training for this first event – the 100-m hurdles – will also benefit the 200 m.

2. High jump
Technique and agility are put to the test in this second event, the high jump. The rules are the same as in the individual event, but the heptathletes are split up into groups of a similar standard. Athletes must ensure that they eat plenty of high-energy food throughout the day, and after the high jump is often a good opportunity to eat.

Day one

Daley Thompson of Great Britain, one of the greatest decathletes ever, is shown in this sequence.

2. Long jump
After the speed of the 100 m, the long jump tests the decathlete's technical ability. Combined event athletes must start each event, or they will be disqualified. However, if they fail to complete the event, for example, by missing a jump, they simply score no points in that event. This could be disastrous for their final score.

3. Shot put
As in the heptathlon, a large physique may be beneficial to this and the other throwing events, but could slow the decathlete down in the sprinting and 1500-m events.

4. High jump
Combined event athletes have to make the best use of their training time, and often train for similar events, such as the long jump, high jump, and the pole vault, at the same time.

1. 100 m
This is the first of the five events completed each day. In the track events, the athletes are allowed three false starts, as opposed to the usual two.

5. 400 m
It is important to drink during the day, but particularly in hot climates and after a strenuous event such as the 400 m. This event is the final one of the first day, and the athletes can look forward to resting before the next day's events.

4. 200 m
This event comes at the end of the first day, when the athlete may be starting to feel tired. It is therefore a test of endurance as well as speed.

Day two

3. Shot put
This event tests an athlete's strength. The distances thrown in the heptathlon are often below those thrown in the individual event because the heptathlete is much lighter, and increasing her body weight for this event could ruin her performance in the other events. Athletes have only three attempts at the throwing events.

5. Long jump
Heptathletes have three attempts at the long jump instead of the usual six. Speed is also vital in this event to ensure a good approach run.

6. Javelin
Technical ability and upper body strength are vital in throwing the javelin. In the individual event, javelin throwers are small and light. Most heptathletes are similarly built and can often pick up a lot of points in this event.

7. 800 m
The key to this final event is endurance rather than speed. By this stage, the heptathlete should be concentrating on winning the points she needs to determine her final score, and should aim to pace herself.

Day two

6. 110-m hurdles
The scores on the second day are often lower as the athletes may be stiff and tired from the previous day. Day two begins with the challenging 110-m hurdles.

9. Javelin
By this stage of the competition, the decathlete will be feeling tired and must concentrate on throwing the javelin accurately to ensure points from this event. With his first "safe" throw, he should aim straight down the middle of the landing area. His second and third throws can then be used to improve the distance achieved.

7. Discus
The discus is often difficult because it requires perfect balance and coordination and the technique is much quicker than the other throwing events.

8. Pole vault
Pole vaulters need to be fast, strong, and flexible to perform the complex series of movements involved in catapulting themselves over a bar using a fiberglass pole.

10. 1500 m
The most grueling event of all, the 1500 m, is the last event. As with the women's 800 m, tactics are more important than speed.

Paralympic Games
Athletes with varying degrees of disabilities compete in the Paralympic Games. Like the Olympics, the Paralympics are held every four years, and wherever possible, they are staged in the same country as the Olympics. The first full Paralympic Games were held in Rome in 1960 and since 1976, the Winter Paralympics have also been held. Events include cycling and judo.

Index

A
Ancient Greek games 5, 20
approach run
  high jump 24
  javelin 28
  long jump 22, 23
  triple jump 20
Athens 5

B
back stretch 5
Barcelona, 1992 Olympics 5
barriers 18
baton, relay 16
bend running 13

C
changeover zone 16
check mark 17
Christie, Linford 12, 16
cleats 7
clothing 6
combined events 30, 31
Conolly, James, 20
cooling down 8
Coubertin, Baron Pierre de 5
cross-country 15
crossover stride 28

D
decathlon 30
dip finish 13
Discobolos 26
discus 26
downsweep pass 17

E
explosive power 10

F
false start 11, 12
Fosbury, Dick 24
Fosbury flop 24
fun run 15

G
grip
  discus 26

javelin 28
shot put 28

H
hang jump 23
heptathlon 30, 31
high jump 24, 25
hill running 15
hitch kick 23
home stretch 5
hurdle heights 18
hurdles 18
hurdles training 19

I
incoming runner 16, 17
infield 5
IOC (International Olympic Committee) 5

J
javelin 28, 29
jumping events 20–25

L
landing area
  high jump 25
  javelin 29
  long jump 23
  shot put 29
linear technique (shot put) 28, 29
long distance events 14
long distance training 14, 15
long jump 22, 23

M
marksman 11
measuring
  javelin 29
  long jump 23
  shot put 29
  triple jump 23
medicine ball 15
middle distance events 14
modern Olympics 18, 20

N
numbers, competition 7

O
O'Brien technique 28
Olympia 5
Olympic flame 5

Olympic games 5
opening ceremony 5
outgoing runner 16, 17
Owens, Jesse 5

R
race walking 15
relay 16
relay baton 16
relay events 16
relay pass
  downsweep 17
  upsweep 17
resistance training 15
rotational technique 28
running events 10–19
runway, javelin 28

S
scissors jump 25
scoring
  decathlon 30, 31
  heptathlon 30, 31
scratch line 29
shot put 28, 29
sprint drills 10
sprinting events 10
standing start 11
start commands 12
starting blocks 12, 13

T
takeoff board 20, 22
takeoff line 20, 22
throwing circle 26–28
throwing events 26–29
track 5
track officials 11
tracksuit 7
training 14
training shoes
  general 6
  specialized 6
triple jump 20–23

U
upsweep pass 17

W
walking *see race walking*
warming up 8

Acknowledgments

DK would like to thank the following people
for their help in the production of this book:

With special thanks to Rez Cameron for his technical input into the book and his expert advice at the photo sessions; all the Young Athletes for their patience and enthusiasm during the photography; Pat Fitzgerald and John Smith of Thames Valley Harriers for their help in organizing the venue, and their support throughout this project; Sarah McClurey for invaluable additional advice on athletics; John Garrett and Paul Ryan for their professionalism and patience throughout the photography; Chetan Joshi for design assistance; Floyd Sayers for organizing the kits.

Picture credits
B=bottom; L=left; R=right; C=center; T=top. The publisher would like to thank the following for their kind permission to reproduce their photographs:
Action Plus/R. Francis 16cr, 31tcr; Tony Henshaw 31bl; Glyn Kirk back cover bl, 4cr, 4bc, 13c; **Agence Vandystadt**/ Laurent Zabulon 31tl; **Allsport**/Tony Duffy front cover bl, inside cover r; Clive Mason front cover tl, 4bl, 15crb; G. Mortimore back cover br, inside cover l, 4tl, 31br; Mike Powell 30tc, 31tr; **Colorsport** 4cl, 11tr, 12t, 18tr, 27cr, 27br, 30bl, 30cl, 30bcl, 30cr, 30bcr, 31bl, 31bcl, 31br, 31bcr; **Mary Evans Picture Library** 5tl, 5ca; **John Hedgethorne** 15br; **Hulton Deutsch Collection** 5cr, 5cl; **Image Bank**/Leo Mason 31tcl; **Mark Shearman** 25tr; **Sporting Pictures** 4br, 5cb, 15bc, 30tr, 31cl.